STEP-BY-STEP™
DRAW
WARRIORS

MARK BERGIN

BOOK HOUSE
a SALARIYA imprint

This edition first published in MMXIX by
Book House

Distributed by Black Rabbit Books
P.O. Box 3263
Mankato, Minnesota 56002

Cataloging-in-Publication Data is available
from the Library of Congress

Printed in the United States
At Corporate Graphics,
North Mankato, Minnesota

9 8 7 6 5 4 3 2 1

ISBN: 978-1-912233-85-4

CONTENTS

MAKING A START

Learning to draw is about looking and seeing. Keep practicing and get to know your subject. Use a sketchbook to make quick drawings. Start by doodling, and experiment with shapes and patterns. There are many ways to draw, and this book shows only some of them. Visit art galleries, look at artists' drawings, see how friends draw, but above all, find your own way.

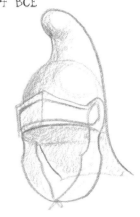

Arcadian hoplite helmet, 364 BCE

Shishak helmet, Ottoman Empire, 1560 CE

Samurai helmet

Spanish sword, 1290 CE

4

Amazonian women fighting

Jambuja
horn-hilt dagger

Drawing models, such as this
one of a Hospitaller knight,
makes good practice.

Take a sketchbook to museums and make
sketches of outfits, armor, and weaponry that
interest you. Make a note of any colors alongside
for future reference.

PERSPECTIVE

If you look at anything from different viewpoints, you will see that the part that is closest to you looks larger, and the part farthest away from you looks smaller. Drawing in perspective is a way of creating a feeling of space—of showing three dimensions on a flat surface.

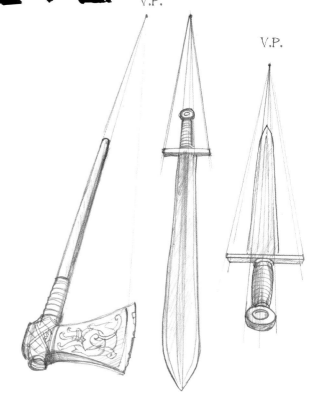

The vanishing point (V.P.) is the place in a perspective drawing where parallel lines appear to meet. The position of the vanishing point depends on the viewer's eye level. Sometimes a low or high viewpoint can give your drawing added drama.

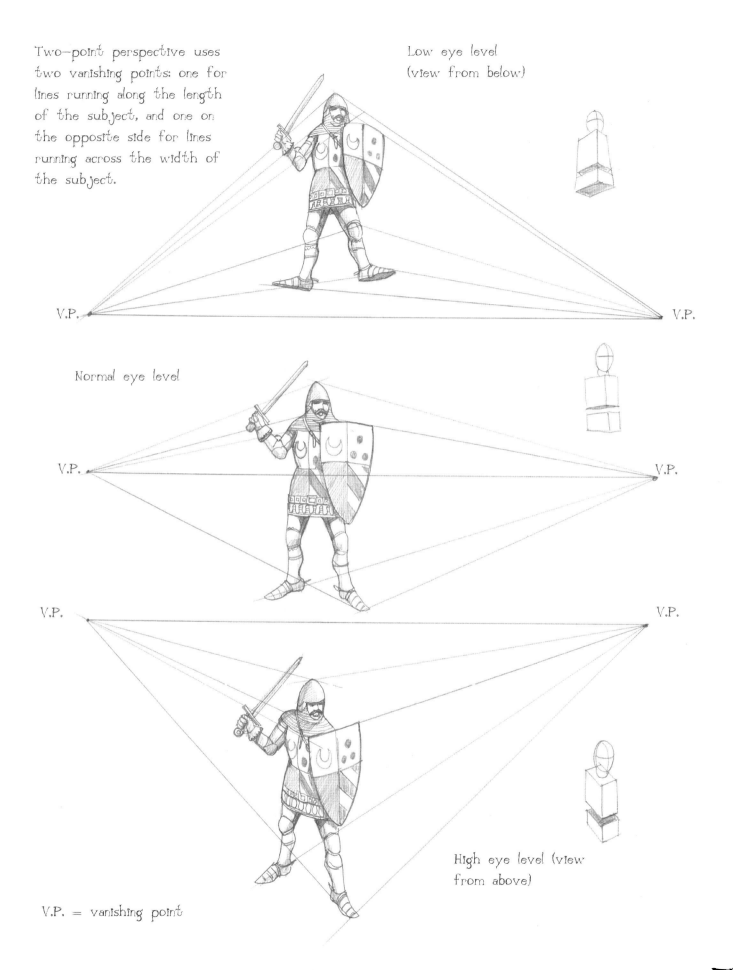

Two-point perspective uses two vanishing points: one for lines running along the length of the subject, and one on the opposite side for lines running across the width of the subject.

Low eye level
(view from below)

Normal eye level

V.P.

V.P.

V.P.

V.P.

V.P.

V.P.

High eye level (view from above)

V.P. = vanishing point

7

DRAWING MATERIALS

Try using different types of drawing paper and materials. Experiment with charcoal, wax crayons, and pastels. All pens, from felt-tips to ballpoints, will make interesting marks—or try drawing with pen and ink on wet paper.

Samurai warrior

Ink silhouette

4th century BCE
Scythian noblewoman

Pencil

Pencil drawings can include a vast amount of detail and tone. Try experimenting with different grades of pencil to get a range of light and shade effects in your drawing.

Remember, the best equipment and materials will not necessarily make the best drawing—only practice will!

8

Felt-tips come in a range of line widths. The wider pens are good for filling in large areas of flat tone.

SAS 22nd Regiment soldier

Ink

Greek hoplite

Felt-tip

Lines drawn in **ink** cannot be erased, so keep your ink drawings sketchy and less rigid. Don't worry about mistakes, as these lines can be lost in the drawing as it develops.

Use solid ink for the very darkest areas and cross-hatching (straight lines criss-crossing each other) for ordinary dark tones. Use hatching (straight lines running parallel to each other) for midtones, and leave the white of the paper for the lightest areas.

ANCIENT GREEK HOPLITE

Hoplites were the citizen—soldiers of the ancient Greek city—states. They carried large, round bronze shields and wore bronze Corinthian helmets that covered nearly the entire head. They also wore bronze greaves on their lower legs. Their body armor was made of stiff linen and bronze scales. They were armed with long spears and swords.

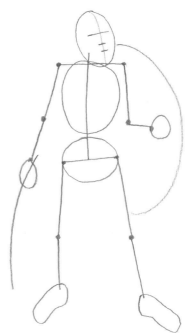

Draw a simple stick figure to define the pose and to position the limbs and joints.

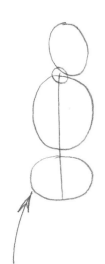

Start by drawing in a large oval for the torso and smaller ovals for the head and hips. Add a center line and a small circle for the neck.

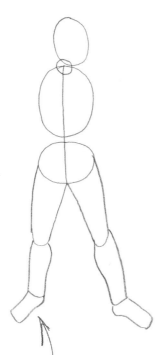

Now, draw in the legs and feet. Indicate the knee and ankle joints.

Draw long ovals for each arm and small ovals for the hands. Indicate all joints.

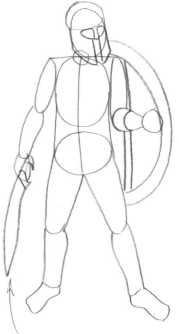

Draw in the helmet, shield, and sword.

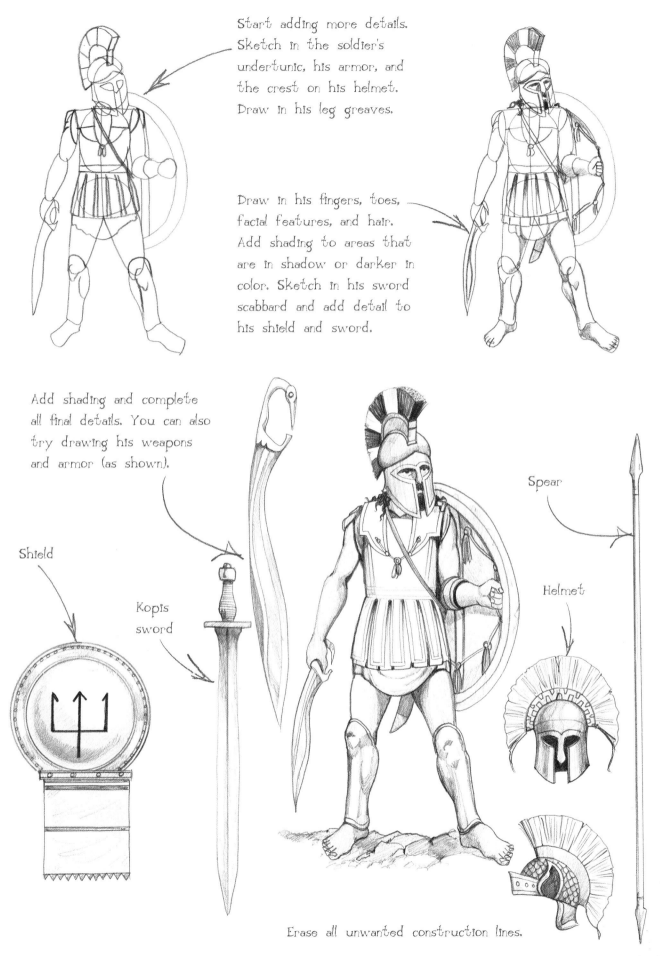

Start adding more details. Sketch in the soldier's undertunic, his armor, and the crest on his helmet. Draw in his leg greaves.

Draw in his fingers, toes, facial features, and hair. Add shading to areas that are in shadow or darker in color. Sketch in his sword scabbard and add detail to his shield and sword.

Add shading and complete all final details. You can also try drawing his weapons and armor (as shown).

Shield

Kopis sword

Spear

Helmet

Erase all unwanted construction lines.

CHINESE IMPERIAL GUARD

Chinese Imperial Guards of the 6th century BCE wore armor made of small bronze plates, which made it difficult to penetrate. They used bronze or iron swords and crossbows that fired a type of arrow called a bolt. A bolt was more likely to pierce armor than an ordinary arrow. The crossbow could be carried ready-loaded.

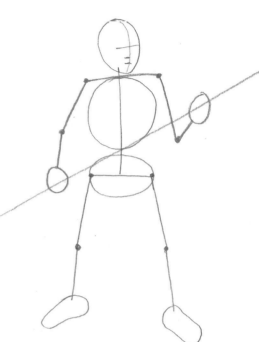

Draw a simple stick figure to define the pose and to position the limbs and joints.

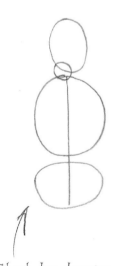

Start by drawing in a large oval for the torso and small ovals for the head and hips. Add a center line and a small circle for the neck.

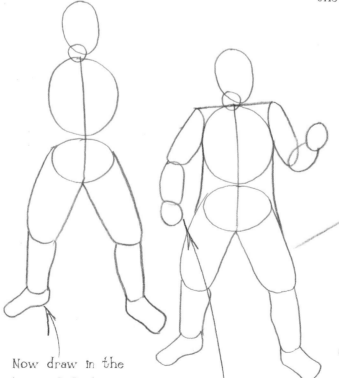

Now draw in the legs and feet. Indicate the knee and ankle joints.

Draw long ovals for each arm and circles for the hands. Indicate all joints.

Add hair and facial features. Sketch in the tunic shape and a line to indicate the pike.

Sketch in his plated body armor and the bindings around his lower legs. Add his footwear.

Draw in the pike blade and its shaft. Add the small plates of armor. Sketch in his fingers. Add shading to areas that are darker in color or in shadow.

Finish off all final details and shading. You can also try drawing his weapons (as shown).

Crossbow and bolt

Erase all unwanted construction lines.

Sword

ROMAN SOLDIER

The size of the Roman Empire meant that its soldiers were almost always off fighting somewhere. Roman soldiers wore metal helmets and body armor. They carried a short, double-edged sword called a gladius, a dagger called a pugio, or javelins called pila, as well as large shields called scutum.

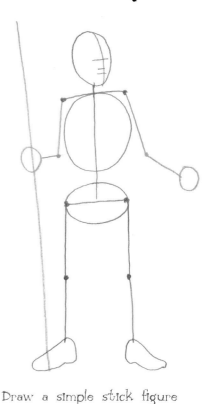

Draw a simple stick figure to define the pose and to position the limbs and joints.

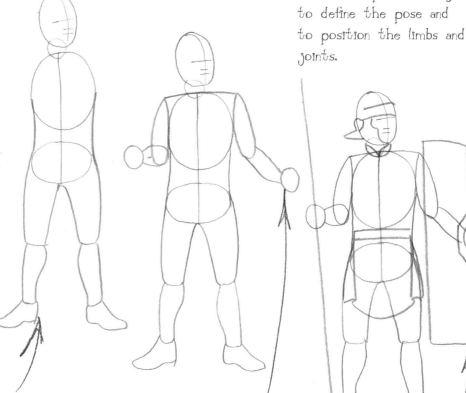

Draw a large oval for the torso and two small ovals for the head and hips. Add a center line and a small circle for the neck. Position the facial features.

Next, draw in the legs and feet. Indicate the knee and ankle joints.

Draw long ovals for each arm and small ovals for the hands.

Sketch in the shape of the soldier's tunic, helmet, shield, and javelin.

Draw in the soldier's protective armor. Add his fingers and his sandals.

Draw in his facial features. Add detail to his armor, the fastenings, and a belt with an apron of studded leather strips. Draw in his sandal straps and shield emblem. Add shading to areas that are darker in color or in shadow.

Add shading and complete all final details. Draw in the ground at his feet. You can also try drawing his weapons and supplies (as shown).

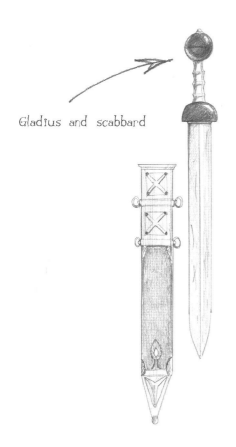

Gladius and scabbard

Erase all unwanted construction lines.

NORMAN KNIGHT

The Norman knights who conquered England in 1066 wore long chain mail coats covering their whole body. Their steel helmets were shaped so that blows from a sword would glance off them. They were armed with a lance for use on horseback, and a sword made of iron and steel for close-quarter combat. They carried wooden shields.

Draw a simple stick figure to define the pose and to position the limbs and joints.

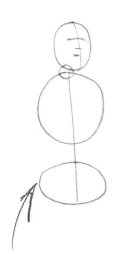

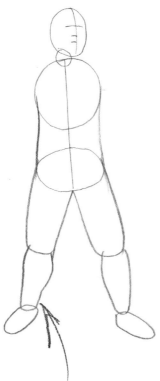

Start by drawing in a large oval for the torso and small ovals for the head and hips. Add a center line and a small circle for the neck. Position the facial features.

Now, draw in the legs and feet. Indicate the knee and ankle joints.

Draw long ovals for each arm and small ovals for the hands. Indicate all joints.

Draw in the soldier's helmet, sword, chain mail coat, and shield.

16

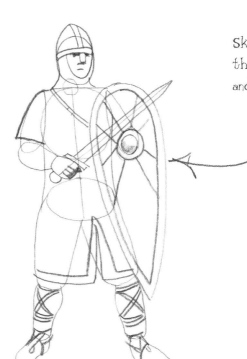

Sketch in the shield design and the binding around his lower legs and feet. Draw in his fingers.

Draw lines to indicate the rows of chain mail. Sketch in his facial features, and add studs to the helmet and shield. Shade in areas that are darker in color or in shadow.

Add shading and complete all final details. Add short wiggly lines to suggest the knitted chain mail. Sketch in tufts of grass at his feet. You can also try drawing his weapons and his shield (as shown).

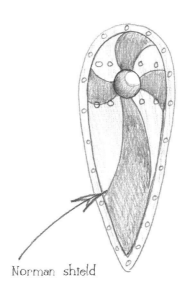

Norman shield

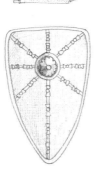

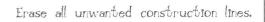

GHULAM CAVALRYMAN

Asian and North African warriors in the Middle Ages often wore chain mail armor and "turban"-style helmets. The saber they carried was a slightly curved, single-edged sword designed to cut better. Their shields were circular, often made from cane, and sometimes decorated.

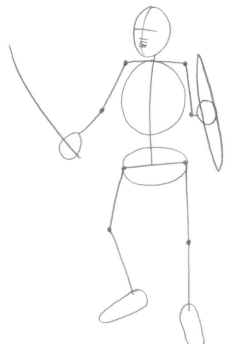

Draw a simple stick figure to define the pose and to position the limbs and joints.

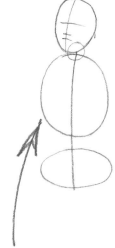

Start by drawing in a large oval for the torso and small ovals for the head and hips. Add a center line and a small circle for the neck. Position the facial features.

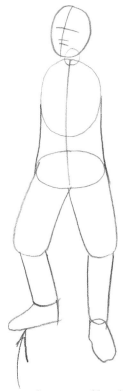

Now draw in the legs and feet. Indicate the knee and ankle joints.

Draw in long ovals for each arm and simple shapes for the hands. Indicate all joints.

Draw in his tunic, helmet, saber, armor, and shield.

18

Draw lines to indicate his plated body armor and add the chain mail sleeves. Sketch in the blade of his saber and add his fingers.

Add a feather to his helmet and sketch in his tunic pattern. Draw the sections of his plated armor. Shade in areas that are darker in color or in shadow.

Close-up of the Ghulam helmet

Complete all details, patterns, and shading, and sketch in the ground he is standing on. You can also try drawing his weapons and his horse (as shown).

Saber

Cavalryman on horseback

Erase all unwanted construction lines.

19

JAPANESE SAMURAI

Samurai was the name of the Japanese warrior class. Their metal armor was lacquered to stop it from rusting in Japan's damp climate. Earlier samurai warriors used the Japanese sword, made of iron and steel, and with a very sharp edge. With the advent of guns in the 15th and 16th centuries, they riveted their armor together to withstand musket balls.

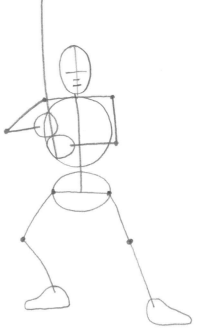

Draw a simple stick figure to define the pose and to position the limbs and joints.

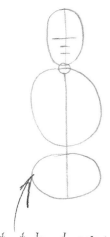

Start by drawing in a large oval for the torso and small ovals for the head and hips. Add a center line and a small circle for the neck. Position the facial features.

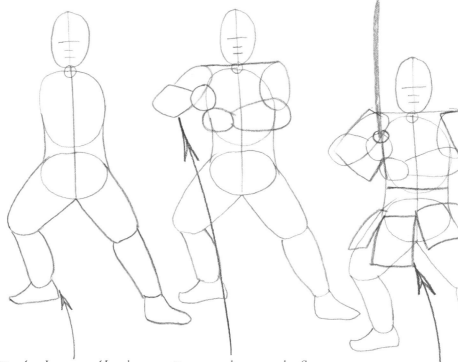

Next, draw in the legs and feet. Indicate the knee and ankle joints.

Draw in long ovals for each arm and small ovals for the hands. Indicate all joints.

Draw in the samurai's sword and the shape of his armor.

20

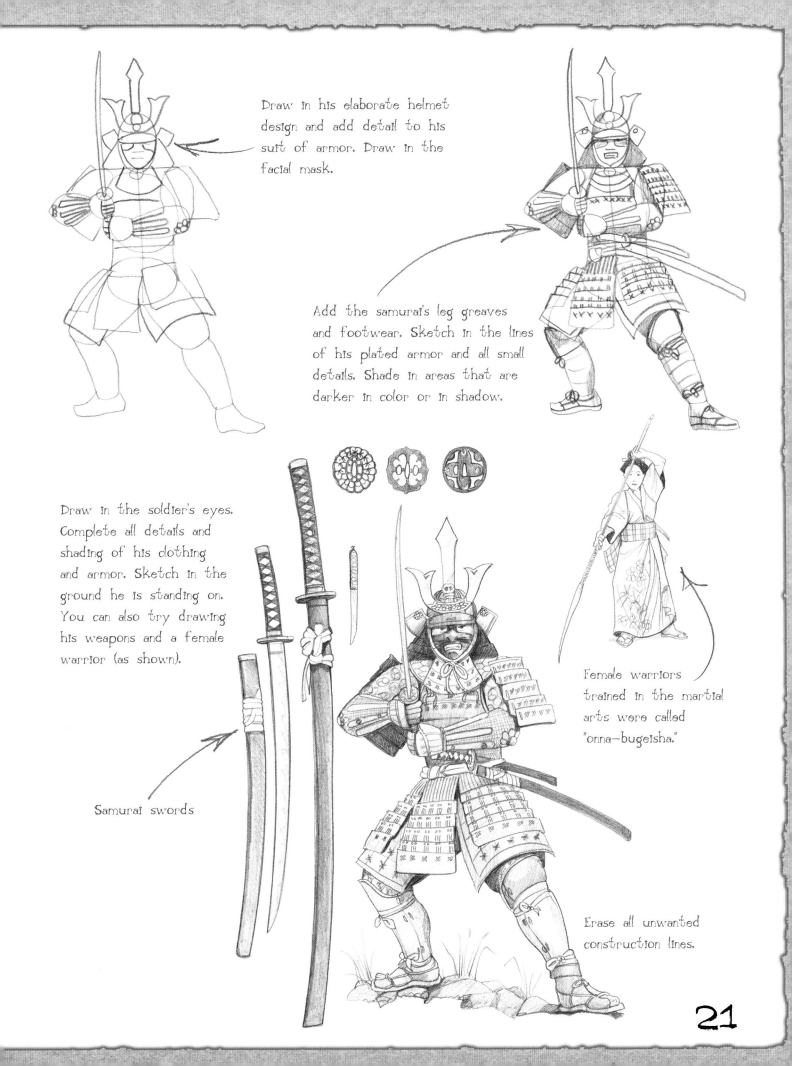

Draw in his elaborate helmet design and add detail to his suit of armor. Draw in the facial mask.

Add the samurai's leg greaves and footwear. Sketch in the lines of his plated armor and all small details. Shade in areas that are darker in color or in shadow.

Draw in the soldier's eyes. Complete all details and shading of his clothing and armor. Sketch in the ground he is standing on. You can also try drawing his weapons and a female warrior (as shown).

Samurai swords

Female warriors trained in the martial arts were called "onna-bugeisha."

Erase all unwanted construction lines.

21

AMERICAN CONTINENTAL SOLDIER

American soldiers in the American War of Independence (1775–1783) wore red uniform jackets and black felt cocked hats. Their flintlock muskets had bayonets to skewer enemy soldiers in close combat.

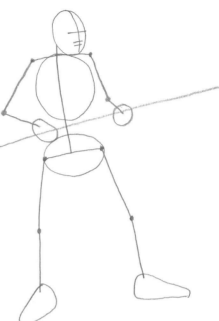

Draw a simple stick figure to define the pose and to position the limbs and joints.

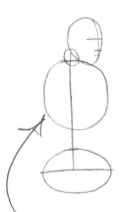

Start by drawing in a large oval and small ovals for the head and hips. Add the center and hip lines, and a small circle for the neck. Position the facial features.

Now, draw in the legs and feet. Indicate the knee and ankle joints.

Draw in long ovals for each arm (note the foreshortening) and small ovals for the hands. Indicate all joints.

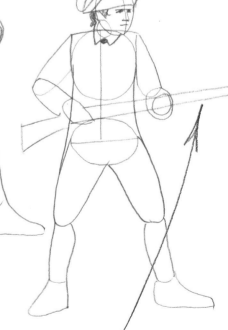

Draw in the soldier's cocked hat, collar, and musket. Add his facial features.

22

Add detail to the soldier's uniform, including buttons and jacket tails. Draw in his ammunition and supply belts.

Draw in the soldier's fingers and footwear. Add a bayonet to his musket. Shade in his hat and all other areas in shadow.

Draw in his face and complete all details and shading. Add tufts of grass at his feet. You can also try drawing his musket and supplies (as shown).

Erase all unwanted construction lines.

INDIAN RAJPUT WARRIOR

Rajput warriors, experts in the Indian martial arts, were trained from birth to become warriors. They wore iron helmets with nose guards, and armor made from leather and chain mail. They were armed with early muskets and curved swords.

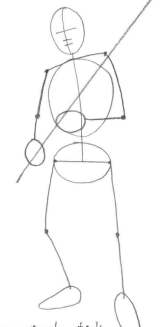

Draw a simple stick figure to define the pose and to position the limbs and joints.

Start by drawing in a large oval for the torso and small ovals for the head and hips. Add the center, hip, and shoulder lines and a small circle for the neck. Position the facial features.

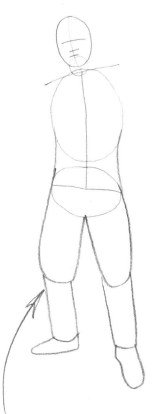

Now, draw in the legs and feet. Indicate the knee and ankle joints.

Draw in long ovals for each arm and small ovals for the hands. Add a line for his musket.

Draw in the shape of his helmet, armor, sword belt, and musket.

Add detail to his armor and helmet. Draw in his facial features, his supply pouch, armguards, and sword.

Add feathers to his helmet and the drapery of his pants. Draw pouches at his waist and add detail to his tunic and sword belt. Add shading to areas in shadow.

Complete all details, patterns, and shading to his clothing. Add final details to his helmet, musket, sword, and scabbard. You can also try drawing his sword (as shown).

NEGATIVE SPACE

Look at the negative space around your drawing as it can alert you to problem areas within the drawing.

Erase all unwanted construction lines.

NAPOLEONIC SOLDIER

Napoléon Bonaparte seized control of the French government in 1799 and declared himself Emperor of France in 1804. In a series of wars of conquest across Europe, India, and the Middle East, his soldiers carried flintlock muskets and sabers, as well as knapsacks containing personal equipment.

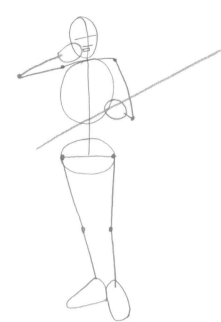

Draw a simple stick figure to define the pose and to position the limbs and joints.

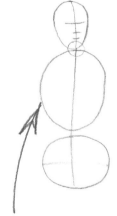

Start by drawing in a large oval for the torso and small ovals for the head and hips. Add the center and hip lines, and a small circle for the neck. Position the facial features.

Next, draw in the legs and feet. Indicate the knee and ankle joints.

Draw in long ovals for each arm and small ovals for the hands.

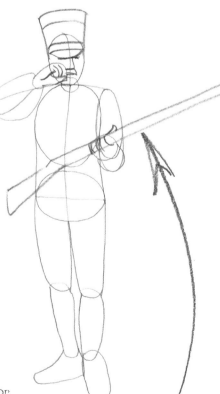

Draw the shape of the soldier's hat and his musket.

26

Start adding details like the soldier's jacket, the components of his musket, and bayonet. Draw in his fingers.

Add his supply belts, jacket buttons, and the garters over his boots. Sketch in the decorative detail on his hat and his knapsack and pouches.

Complete all final details of his uniform. Finish off his facial features and add shading to areas that are darker in color or in shadow. Add grass around his feet. You can also try drawing him from behind, or try separate drawings of his saber and supplies (as shown).

Saber

21

Erase all unwanted construction lines.

AMERICAN CIVIL WAR SOLDIER

Union soldiers in the Civil War from 1861–1865 wore dark–blue woolen jackets and light–blue woolen pants. They carried muskets, often with bayonets attached, a water bottle, and a knapsack to hold cartridge boxes and a bedroll.

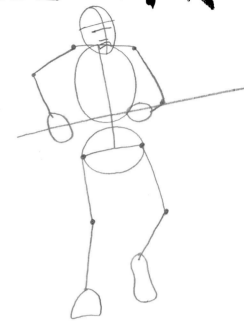

Draw a simple stick figure to define the pose and to position the limbs and joints.

Start by drawing in a large oval for the torso and small ovals for the head and hips. Add the center and hip lines, and a small circle for the neck. Position the facial features.

Now, draw in the legs and feet. Indicate the knee and ankle joints.

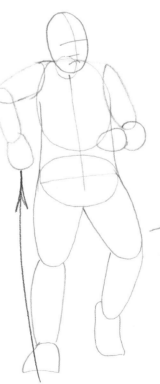

Draw in long ovals for each arm (note the foreshortening) and small ovals for the hands.

Add the shape of the soldier's cap, uniform, and musket.

28

Draw the facial features. Add a knapsack, supply belts, and boots. Draw the fingers.

Draw in the component parts of the soldier's musket and add shading to areas in shadow.

Draw in the soldier's face, including his stubble. Add all finishing touches and the detail around his feet. Shade in areas that are darker in color. You can also try drawing the smaller figure below or the musket detail (as shown).

Musket

Erase all unwanted construction lines.

Confederate soldier

29

SAS TROOPER

The modern British army soldier has close-fitting body armor that is easier to move in. Their helmets are fitted with weapon sights and night-vision goggles. They are armed with pistols and assault rifles.

Draw a simple stick figure to define the pose and to position the limbs and joints.

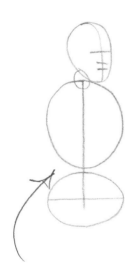

Start by drawing in a large oval for his torso and small ovals for the head and hips. Add a center and hip line, and a small circle for the neck. Position the facial features.

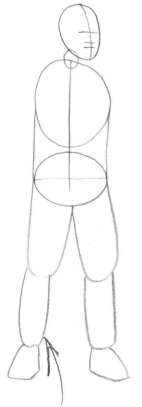

Next, draw in the legs and feet. Indicate the knee and ankle joints.

Draw in long ovals for each arm and small ovals for the hands.

Draw in the soldier's rifle and his helmet with its weapon sights.

Now draw in his jacket and add supply pouches to his body armor. Sketch in his fingers and scarf.

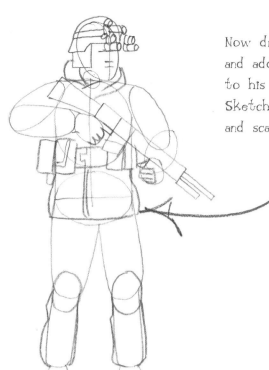

COMPOSITION

Composition is the arrangement of an image on paper. Consider which format improves your drawing—an upright (portrait) format or a horizontal (landscape) format.

Now start adding more detail. Draw in the pockets on his jacket, his boots, kneepads, and the equipment strapped to his legs.

Complete all shading and details. Add the khaki pattern to his uniform. You can also try drawing his gas mask (as shown).

Erase all unwanted construction lines.

31

GLOSSARY

Composition   The arrangement of the parts of a picture on the drawing paper.

Construction lines   Guidelines used in the early stages of a drawing; they may be erased later.

Cross-hatching   The use of criss-crossed lines to indicate dense shade in a drawing.

Foreshortening   Reducing the size or distorting the shape of part of an object in order to create the illusion that the object is in three-dimensional space and is being seen from the perspective of the viewer.

Greaves   Pieces of armor worn over the shins.

Hatching   The use of parallel lines to indicate light and shade in a drawing.

Musket   An early type of firearm. The bullets and gunpowder would be loaded directly into the end of the gun's barrel.

Negative space   The empty space around all parts of a drawing, often an important part of the composition.

Perspective   A method of drawing in which near objects are shown larger than faraway objects to give an impression of depth.

Silhouette   A drawing that shows only a flat dark shape, like a shadow.

INDEX